To Fight Fire with Sun

To Fight Fire with Sun

D. A. Andrews

Cover Art and Illustrations by Roux.

ISBN: 978-0-5788-1764-4

*For Alexander, I remember telling you
that one day I would dedicate a book to you.
This one is for you.
Forever with love, Davia*

PREFACE

For as long as I can remember, I have used the beauty of words to process my innermost feelings. From scribbling in journals to writing short stories for competitions to honing my craft in Ms. Shirley's poetry course at the University of the West Indies, my inner child has used words to delve into the problem at hand (or as a form of escape from the trials of this lifetime).

I have known loss through a plethora of experiences. Whether I lost friends, lovers, or myself, I somehow came back to poetry no matter how many times I wandered away. This book was born from one of the most significant losses of my life: that of my dear friend Alexander.

In the pages that follow, I share with you parts of me that very few have seen. I shared some of these poems with their intended party. Some were shared with loved ones. Some have only now seen the light of day. It is in sharing our hardest trials that we can feel closer and connected.

If life has taught me anything, it is that to live the human experience is to know pain. I do not wish to sugar coat anything or romanticize any form of depression or mental illness. I, simply, hope to share with you what got me through certain moments. With that being said, I do issue some sort of trigger warning for the following pages. I have dealt with great hurt, and some of these poems may leave a bitter taste in one's mouth and a heavy weight on one's heart. But I hope that you can know that you are not alone in the dark night of your soul. I hope you can find a phrase or sentence that has been written here that helps you feel as though your experience is represented. For, we must feel our feelings in this lifetime, whether "good," "bad," or "ugly." It is in these hardships of life that we deeply appreciate what is in front of us.

I wish you well on this journey you have chosen on the planet Earth and hope that you find solace in something the way I have found it in words.

With love and light,

D. A. Andrews

ACKNOWLEDGMENTS

To Courtney-Claire Haynes, you have been my refuge and strength from the moment we got close at the local university. Your constant, unwavering support has kept me going throughout the years. Whether you stood by me through losing lovers, friends, or myself, there has been an undeniable sense of friendship, sisterhood, and love that traveled across the distance. I am forever grateful to have you in my life, and I hope to continue to grow with you in many years to come. Those rocking chairs will not rock themselves!

To Cheresh Smallwood, when I look at you, I see one of the strongest women I have ever met. You amaze me daily with how much support, love, and care you give to the people in your life. I am grateful to have met you and that I ran into that bathroom that day. Thank you for being one of my beta readers in the initial stages of this body of work. Thank you for always supporting me. Thank you for always having my back. Thank you for never kicking me out of "our" apartment.

To Savitri Tolan, you have been one of my greatest supporters since we met. You have always pushed me to write a book and have continuously made me feel loved and supported, no matter how many miles separated us. I am forever grateful to Facebook for bringing us together and am eternally thankful for you for being a part of my life. Keep shining on with your love, light, dances, and writing. I love you.

To Lindsey Leigh Harper and Rebecca Johnson, thank you for your kindness and for volunteering to be beta readers for this. Without your input in this, I would not be as far as I am today. I appreciate you both as being fellow writers and fellow members of the Scribbler community. Thank you for your feedback and support.

To Alexander Lyn, I feel your presence as I write this. I feel your love pour into my body, and I feel you cheering me on in the process. I hope to shine a light in this world the way you have shone the sun into everyone you had encountered. I hope to "embrace ridiculousness" the way you did, in such a way that you saw the good in life while things went downhill. You are one of my greatest muses. Thank you for being my guide, my teacher, my friend.

*Living each day, which is
connected to the past and
leads to the future; a future built
off the past, tiled with the present
which we aren't guaranteed to live in.
So, instead of trying to roof the life
you live in, why not live it openly
and stare at the stars.*

-Alexander J. D. Lyn

Let Love Live On

TO FIGHT FIRE WITH SUN

He holds loyalty as close
to his chest as the people
he keeps there; foraging
through his ribs for every
ounce of strength to
give to others.

Sows light into
those that are trapped
in the arms of darkness;
almost as golden
as the specks that shine
in his eyes.

He does this, for he
measures his life by
the cups of himself
he pours into those that
need it, and the pounds
of pain he has endured
over the years.

Because to fight fire
with fire, one must know
the tactics of the enemy.
But to fight fire with sun
encompasses the hardships
he has overcome.

NECKLACE

My hand religiously moves to the space
between my breasts; fingers feel
for pendant against sternum.

It suspends from chain-links, hangs
securely around my neck; its twin
adorns another.

Fussing with the flattened ring, my thumb
glides over the inscription: "Love"
etched into stainless steel. Sealed
with cubic zirconia, this lighthouse
still guides me towards outstretched arms.

Like an old album, it carries
memories of pleated skirts, fingers
touching insides of thighs, secrets
passed from mouth to ear, love
between two girls.

GREEN ACRES, SPANISH TOWN

I make my way through the maze
of two-storey houses, trek on red earth,
pass balconies stilted on the side of a hill,
up to a home with overgrown hedges
and forest-green awnings.

I stand outside the white-washed door,
my hand hovering just before the brass knob,
about to enter a place where our bodies
often collided on a Queen-sized mattress.

I am greeted by the familiar smell
of white rum and Coco Chanel #5.
I am here to visit her, see this woman
I haven't seen in two months.

Her drawings: cats, houses, children,
adorn the eggshell-white walls. Life breathes
through medals displayed around mirrors,
photographs tucked between wood and glass.

Cards scatter as we play War, "You know
I'm going to win," "I'd like to see you try."
Our laughter drowned out by the whir
of a white Panasonic fan.

IMMACULATE CONCEPTION
After Paul Hostovsky

You aren't supposed to touch,
except on days when you're herded into chapel,
allowed to mark a cross on her forehead with ash.
The nuns hover like hawks, keep you in queues,
arms-length apart, "two-a-breast."
But, when you do, touch her the way you would
piano keys during Beethoven's fifth:
aggressively, energetically, quickly.
Make use of moments spent in class devotions,
heads bowed as they recite the Lord's prayer.
Linger when you reach into her pocket at lunch,
say you need to borrow money,
slide your finger through the hole
she made the night before,
brush thumb against the skin of her thigh, smile.
Put your hand on her back when you ask
to borrow a pen; leave it there while you wait.
Ask to go to the nurse after she's excused
for the bathroom, meet her in the last stall;
be mindful of wandering eyes and cleaning ladies.

THE HUNT

He is clothed in strength,
though thoughts race
day by day.

Armoured in green
with never much to say.
Unwavering confidence
and the brightest smile
he suffers in silence
mile by mile.

I have looked up to him
from the moment we met,
entranced by a gaze
we shared across that
living room carpet.

But with every problem
he faces there,
I pray and hope
he knows I am here.

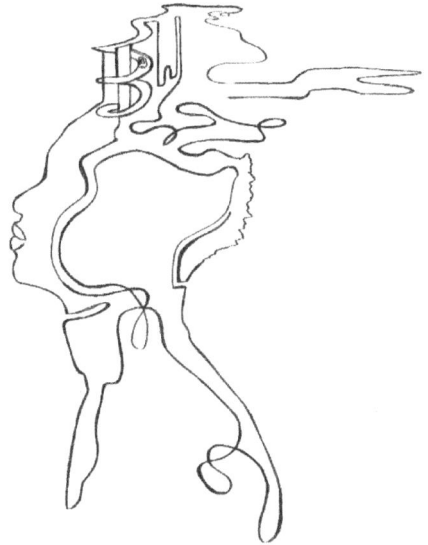

HOW IT BEGAN

He sits next to me, arms
pulling his legs closer,
lips widen into smile as
others dare him to kiss me.

His back straightens, his head
higher than before. I notice
the way his hair is always messy
and focus on his lips as
a simple "no problem" spills
from them.

He inches closer to me,
I, closer to him. The space
between our lips diminishing
until mine welcomes his.
We are to hold this embrace
for no less than a minute.

Somewhere, a voice beckons,
hands pull at my shoulder,
another pair at his,
crying for an end to this.

But explain to me,
how do you tell a dying man
to stop breathing after he
has had the sweet taste of air?

BRAVERY

So, love me out loud,
for I have been kept
hidden inside sealed lips
like a secret, shunned
as if a scarlet letter
had been placed
on my chest.

I am tired and crave
a love that allows
me the courtesy
of being me:
open, wild, free.

So,
love me without restriction,
love me without guilt,
love me for me.
Love me with patience
and keep that fire
fueled.
Love me out loud,
love me out loud.
Love
Me
Out
Loud.

HORIZON

As far back as I can remember,
the beach has been my safe
space. Though I have never
ventured out to shore often,
those few moments there
brought stillness and appreciation
for this Earth we call home.

I learned along the way
never to create a home
in other people, especially
when home often was
the place I fell asleep.

But I learned to admire
the horizon and its ability
to instill hope when you
were at the end of your rope.

I look at you and all I see is
the opportunity for love,
happiness,
support.

And even though homes
are just buildings where
we rest our heads at night,
horizons can be created
by a simple glance
across a crowded room.

ICEBREAKER

She holds Orion's Belt
on her left shoulder,
the rest of the universe
on her right.

She kisses with conviction,
is sure and firm,
but still manages to be
soft in the process.

Her arms, a safety net,
ushering those that dwell
in them to unravel
without feeling undone.

Her heart has the courage
to always love once more,
no matter how many times
it has been left behind.

She breaks and rebuilds,
stares into reflective surfaces,
hopes to see the light
that once was.

For, to know her is to know
God and to love her is,
undeniably,
an experience of a lifetime.

THE SNAKE PLANT

Sylvie's leaves yellow around
the edges. Still, she stands tall
in the blue octagon pot
I buried her roots in.

She moves from living
room table to back porch
depending on light; lowers
her leaves to signal her needs.
I have grown to understand
exactly how to show her love.

The edges of your lips
turn down quickly when
you ponder. You, ultimately,
decide silence is a better
answer; shrug shoulders
and move on to the next.

I catch you staring
at me often, feel pull as
you rush past, understand when
you hold other's problems
close to your chest in hopes
of giving yourself purpose.

And though I have grown
to take care of this other living
thing, feed love to you in parking
lots and quick glances, I grow
shy to let those words
spill from my lips.

Before I Let You Go

CYCLES

I have embraced solitude like
an old friend. Mustered up
enough courage to hold its hand
on days I feel everything.

I sit by the phone waiting
for you to see me. Tell myself
I am okay with its silence,
that if you text
I will wait;
not appear to be desperate.

I sit by the phone
waiting for you to see me.
Tell myself that
I have embraced solitude
like an old friend.

−I just want you to want me again

COMPULSIONS

I count my teeth each day
like clockwork; smooth finger
over each one, calling out its position
like children's names in roll call.

My mother warns me
against stepping on cracks.
A pervasive attempt
at covering her ass
in this uncertain world;
she urges me never
to set foot Downtown.

His name appears every day
as if it has become a part of me.
I see it in the way
the father crosses his child
along the highway.
I see it when I cut my own bangs
and when the clock strikes
that number that is bare-boned as him.

I count my teeth
like clockwork each day,
trying to see if the teeth
that awkwardly clashed
against his are still intact.

It is my attempt at saving
all I have left of him.

NAMES

I don't care for nicknames.

Not with respect to the shortened versions of your name, but the ones that are simple phrases in our language.

I never cared to see, speak, write, or call you by an ordinary word.

I used to think it made it less personal (less loving) to call you a name that everyone else did.

I took to only calling you by the name on your birth certificate; I took pleasure in being the only one.

I used to think this was the reason I never called you the name others called you.

It was not until you walked away that I understood why.

I detest nicknames born from ordinary words in the dictionary.

Because no matter how often I try to forget you, I stumble into you each day.

SILENCE

I become silent,
answer texts less,
turn my phone off,
become absorbed
by blankets and pillows.

Now, I stare at blank pages.
For what was meant to be
filled with words, is only
occupied by lines; empty
like the land from where
this book was born.

The last thing
I opened my mouth to say
was I love you.
The last thing
you gave me was a sad look
as you knew this was the end.

I've become silent,
limiting my time spent with words
Because how do you open
your mouth to even breathe,
when the last time you did
made you lose everything?

MY THERAPIST TAUGHT ME HOW TO GROUND MYSELF

I practice saying goodbye
in the mirror each day.
Hold my shoulders back,
move my hair out of my eyes,
as if this gives me strength.

I run my tongue across my teeth,
sink feet into floor,
take deep breaths,
and hope the senses
are enough to ground me.

Sirens wailing
in the distance are enough
to bring me back into the moment,
unaware of how my shoulders
had caved in on themselves,
and how my hair stood on end.

I practice saying goodbye
to you each day,
as if it will prepare me
for when my heart breaks.

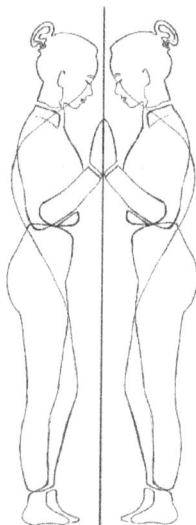

–Sometimes practice does not make perfect

I find myself begging for a broken heart. I consume images of you and her together, your baby (that should have been mine) propped on her knee. She stands taller than I do, cooks more, cleans more, and is not riddled with all manner of compulsions.

In theory, she is better for you. She supplies stability and that "unbroken" family you have craved for since your eyes were at your knees. So, I stare at the stories, see your wedding pictures, see the flowers you send her over and over in hopes that my heart breaks quickly.

Maybe I can pick up the pieces and build a new home.

The hardest thing
I have ever had to do
was watch
the love of my life
make a home with
another wife.

–Heartbreak can be hidden by a smile

HOW WE MOVE ON

I scrub my skin religiously,
drag loofah against it
the way school children
roll around in dirt: aggressively
and without much thought.

I zone out
each of the four times
I engage in this ritual.
Understand that
these are the moments
you no longer exist.

For those 5 minutes and 42 seconds,
my mind's eye is occupied
with the way the bubbles
pile over themselves, how lavender
mixes with sweat, and the sound water
makes as it flows down the drain.

I use this as a means to an end:
a seemingly mundane task
becomes the way I remove
your touch from my skin.

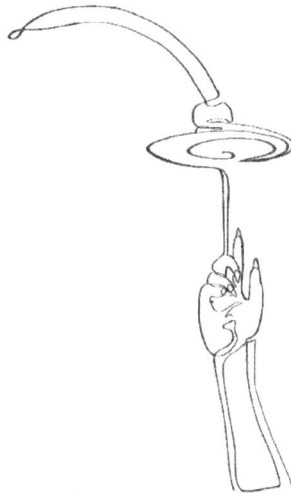

ALEXANDER

I find myself reaching
for the phone
as this is one of the last
places you inhabit.

I replay your recording, run
my fingers over my eyes,
thumb over my temples
as your voice echoes on repeat.

You wanted to escape,
not be burdened to bed.
Your voice cracking
as somehow you knew
it would come to this.

I hear your voice
in my head every hour,
feel static run across my palms,
knowing you have reached
across the veil to still
be my comfort.

But time cannot heal
the hole you left in our hearts.
Because how do you let go
of something so beautiful,
when all it ever taught you
was to hold on?

-Through good times and bad, all we must do is hold on

UNTOLD STORIES FROM AN AIR MATTRESS

He uses alcohol
to escape his pain.
I sit in bed beside him
wondering
if it hurts more for me
to be there or not.

He takes another sip,
blasts Kendrick
and speaks to himself
incessantly
about his daily activities.

I sit here looking out
the glass pane,
notice the leaves falling
and wonder if
he is as obsessively aware
of the short time
that we have left as I am.

With every second drawing
closer to the day I leave,
my mind runs frantic.
I look over at him
and he pops open another beer.

–Someone should have told you, you can't drown your sorrows

LIFE IS NOT ALWAYS FAIR

Morning breaks each day
at the most inopportune time.
I roll over, trying to grasp for
the last few seconds before
alarms blare against the walls.

He clothes himself in
worries and camouflage,
while I take in each second,
counting the days down
until 4500 miles separate us.

Each day that passes
is another day closer
to when they move in.
And for them,
morning would break
at the most opportune time.

Quite often, home has become a choice
of where I unload my car at the end of the night.
I have gotten quite good at leaving things in
and living out of suitcases.

NO LONGER A STEADY GAZE

I unearth anxiety
from my wounds, try to
muster up enough courage
to look over at you.

You and I
have crossed paths
multiple times,
never really stopping
just short enough to
exist on the same timeline.

After one night
of wine and passion,
our game began with
forbidden glances and
the chase of a lifetime:
what once was never
became something more.

And just as quickly
as it began, it ended
just hours after my head laid
on your chest. For you chose
another: unaware of my feelings,
denying your own.

So, tell me,
how do I go on
looking at you?

I write people into poems
in hopes this is the way
they live on.

TUESDAY

A half-filled bowl sits
in front of me,
on the white-washed
wooden table
which seats four.

The only other being
to accompany me
this morning is
Sylvie, the potted
snake plant I got
two years ago from
some woman
on the side of the road.

The air in my apartment
is stale today;
the four-day-old oatmeal
in my blue bowl
competing with it
for first place.

I sit at this spot each day,
thinking up some sort of
partner to join us.
Each time, my mind
brings me back to you.

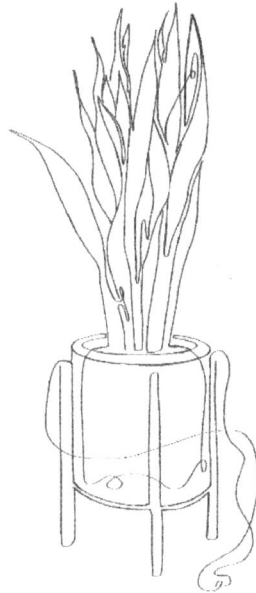

ALMOST

He lays on top of me,
hair falls, framing what
I can make out of his face
in this dimly lit room.

Light flickers against his
brown skin (about five shades
darker than yours), light
brown eyes grow hazel
as candle flames dance.

His bones protrude from his skin
(like yours), he hovers over me
like you do (did?), lets "good girl"
fall out of his lips almost
as well as you.

But though the light turns his eyes
the same shade as yours, they don't
look at me the way yours do,
his face isn't clean-shaven, fingers
don't dance against my back like yours.

We are taught to cherish moments,
hold them as carefully as an egg, stay
in the present, for we know not
what the future holds.

But as I look up, stare at the shadows
flickering across the ceiling,
feel beard scratch against my thighs,
I wonder if I will ever stop looking
for you in all the wrong places.

THE GOLDEN MIRROR

She looks at me
with eyes lacking candor,
scoops hair into bun, thumbs
palm with a sense of unease.

Her mouth parts then
closes as quickly as it
opened, as if she hears
silencing before anyone
has gotten the chance to utter it.

Her gaze averts my own,
mine avert hers, we sit
across from each other,
encapsulated by clouds
of anxiety, knees drawing
further into chest, light in
eyes flickering away.

I sit there, staring at a version
of me which no longer
exists, see the child
that has built walls
against the world.

Understand that broken
people take time to heal,
and losing yourself
gives your soul a chance
to be found.

RITUAL

I collect worries, pocket
them as one would sea glass.
The load has become as
unbearable as the days; feet
dragging slower and slower
as time ticks.

With each passing minute,
the thought becomes
clearer. I sit cross-legged
at the brown coffee table,
usher candles into holders, tie
cord around width.

With intention, the load
is deposited. Tears fall,
leave marks on cheeks,
carrying with it the weight
of what once was.

Wick is lit, wax pools, drips
down the red one first,
white one next. As flame
burns brighter, the candle
burns lower, releasing us
in the process.

For we were not meant
to last longer than we were.
And as cord breaks, I stop
carrying you around as
love that was almost.

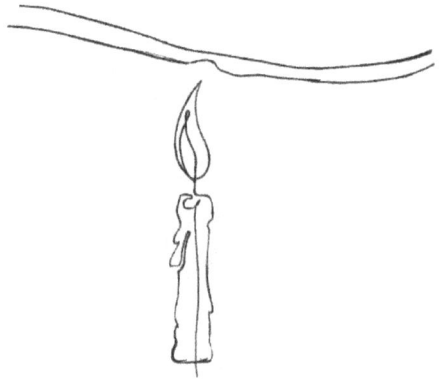

To Fight Fire with Sun

Thank you for taking the time to read this book.

I hope that you enjoyed it and ask that you
leave a review if you feel compelled to.

If you would like to follow me on
my writing and day-to-day journey
you can find me on
Instagram @dayandrews_

With love & light,

D. A. Andrews

ABOUT THE AUTHOR

D. A. Andrews was born and raised in Kingston, Jamaica. Throughout the years, she has developed wide interests in various aspects of life, such as coffee, weddings, books, and psychology. She is a graduate of the University of the West Indies, Mona Campus with a BSc. in Marine Biology and Psychology (Honours) and is currently pursuing her MBA. She considers herself a nomad at heart and has changed cities and apartments quite as often as she changes her clothes. She is currently resting her head in Brunswick, Georgia, with her black cat (and familiar), Luna. To Fight Fire with Sun is her debut collection of poems.

www.ingramcontent.com/pod-product-compliance
Lightning Source LLC
Chambersburg PA
CBHW021921040426
42448CB00007B/851